DEDICATION

This journal is dedicated to YOU, a
young dreamer and creator, who is
going to improve the world.

We believe in you.

This journal is available at special quantity discounts for bulk
purchase. For details, write to support@biglifejournal.com

Printed in the United Kingdom

www.biglifejournal.com
ISBN: 978-0-578-51712-4

Second Edition

THIS JOURNAL
belongs to

_____

MY JOURNAL BUDDY IS

_____

WE STARTED THIS JOURNAL ON (DATE)

_____

What is
BIG LIFE JOURNAL?

- Big Life Journal is for you to explore your ideas and thoughts and enjoy the special time with your JOURNAL BUDDY.

- In this journal, you will discover how to believe in yourself, why being unique is important, ways to share kindness with others, and much more!

- Big Life Journal will also help you develop a **growth mindset** (your hidden superpower)! It's a great thing to have because with a growth mindset, you can learn anything and achieve any goal!

- When you have a growth mindset, you believe you can always improve by making an effort and using the right strategies.

How to use BIG LIFE JOURNAL

Choose your JOURNAL BUDDY

Invite someone to be your JOURNAL BUDDY. It can be a parent, a grandparent, or anyone else you want to share this special journal with.

Pick a time each week

Find a time that works for you and your JOURNAL BUDDY every week to sit down with your Big Life Journal.

Listen to the Big Life Kids podcast

Listen to the episodes as you're going through the journal. The episodes align with the chapters and have extended versions of the stories. You can subscribe to the podcast wherever you get your podcasts.

A special note for the
JOURNAL BUDDY

- Big Life Journal is a connection tool which provides you with an opportunity to discuss important topics with your child, even when life gets busy.

- Your child will mirror your attitude towards the journal. Treat your Big Life Journal time as a fun and relaxed activity. When you show excitement, your child will be curious and will want to know why.

- If your child is reluctant to write — write it for them! The conversations you will have and their overall understanding of the topics are much more important.

- We hope the time you spend together on this journal will become a special time you both cherish and look forward to.

What's inside

There are 10 chapters, each broken into two parts.

All About Me and My Superpowers............................8

1. Believe in Yourself.................................11

2. Mistakes Help You Grow.............................27

3. Be Persistent.......................................43

4. Be Grateful..59

5. Be Unique, Be You..................................75

6. Challenges Make You Stronger.......................91

7. Effort is Key..................................... 107

8. Love Learning.....................................123

9. Be Kind.. 139

10. Make a Difference in the World....................155

At the end of each chapter, there's a colouring page. When you complete all chapters, cut the colouring pages out, arrange them in a grid, then tape them to a poster board to create your own unique poster!

ALL ABOUT ME

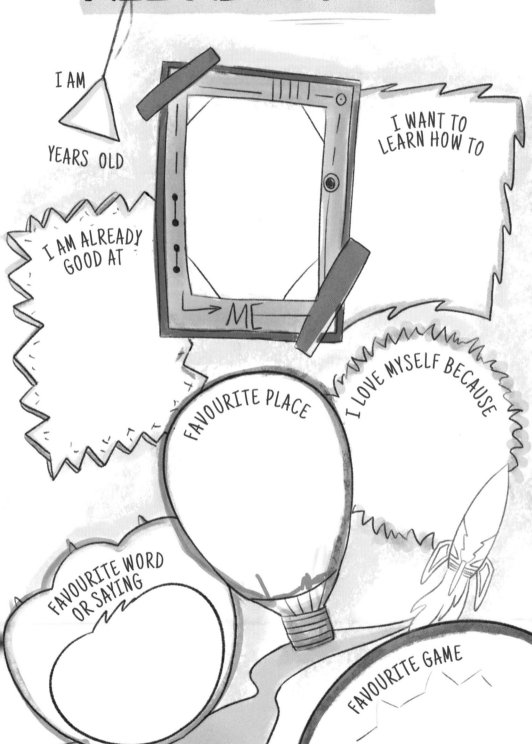

MY SUPERPOWERS

Check the boxes below

- ☐ My kindness
- ☐ My imagination
- ☐ I can learn anything
- ☐ My powerful brain
- ☐ I make cool things
- ☐ I never give up
- ☐ My funny jokes
- ☐ I am a good friend
- ☐ I help others
- ☐ My great ideas
- ☐ I love to dance
- ☐ I can do anything
- ☐ _____
- ☐ _____
- ☐ _____

9

PART I

Believing in yourself means trusting yourself and doing your best to achieve your goals. It makes you stronger and more likely to succeed.

 Ask your JOURNAL BUDDY about a time when believing in themselves helped them through a difficult situation.

Think of a story character from your favourite book or film. Write the character's name below.

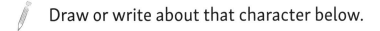

Think of a time when the character believed in themselves. Share the story with your JOURNAL BUDDY.

Draw or write about that character below.

you
CAN DO
HARD
things

You can do hard things

Keep Dreaming and Believing

Our story begins in a landfill in Cateura, Paraguay. Every day, big lorries bring the city's garbage to this landfill. Once the rubbish has been dumped, the landfill workers pick through it, trying to find metal and plastic bottles to sell. Working at the landfill is hot and dangerous, and often makes the workers very ill.

When an environmental engineer named Favio came to Cateura, he realised that as long as the city continued to throw away so much rubbish, the landfill would continue to grow.

The rubbish was destroying the environment; the Paraguay River was filthy and filled with plastic bags and containers. Most children were destined to become gancheros, or rubbish pickers, just like their parents. Favio, however, believed he could still make a difference. He decided to give free music lessons.

Soon there were children of all ages lining up to learn. But Favio didn't have enough instruments for them all. A new violin was worth more than a house in Cateura.

Colá, a landfill worker, visited Favio, and asked, "Do you think we could make the instruments?" Favio knew they had no money, and no equipment...what would they make instruments out of? Colá had the answer. "What do we have more of than anything else?!" he asked Favio. "Garbage!"

It took a lot of trial and error to get the instruments just right. Oven trays became violins; huge oilcans became cellos and double basses. Saxophones and flutes were made from bottle tops and drainpipes!

Many people laughed at Colá's idea — but Colá believed in himself, and the children of Cateura believed in him too. Favio and Colá soon realised they had made real musical instruments, fit for an orchestra, from rubbish. And so, the orchestra **Los Reciclados** was born.

Favio taught the students to focus on the actions that helped them to achieve positive results. This meant lots of practice, but it also meant learning the importance of believing in themselves. You see, when the students doubted themselves, the instruments didn't sound good. And although they didn't feel confident about the music they were playing, because it was new and unknown, they needed to feel confident about themselves.

After countless hours of practice, Los Reciclados received an invitation to play in Rio de Janeiro, Brazil. Though they felt they weren't ready to play in front of a huge audience, their performance was a huge success. Soon after, they performed in the USA, Netherlands, Norway, Canada, and Japan!

They even toured across South America with Metallica, one of the greatest heavy metal bands of all time. The world had discovered that children in Paraguay could make magic out of rubbish! Los Reciclados proved if you work hard and believe in yourself, you can fulfil your biggest dreams — you can live your biggest life!

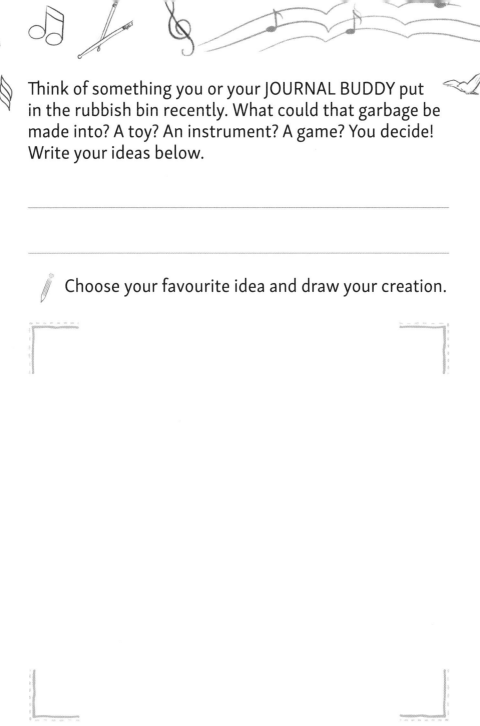

Think of something you or your JOURNAL BUDDY put in the rubbish bin recently. What could that garbage be made into? A toy? An instrument? A game? You decide! Write your ideas below.

_____

_____

Choose your favourite idea and draw your creation.

Can you make your idea a reality and actually turn that piece of garbage into something new? Try it with your JOURNAL BUDDY now!

PART 2

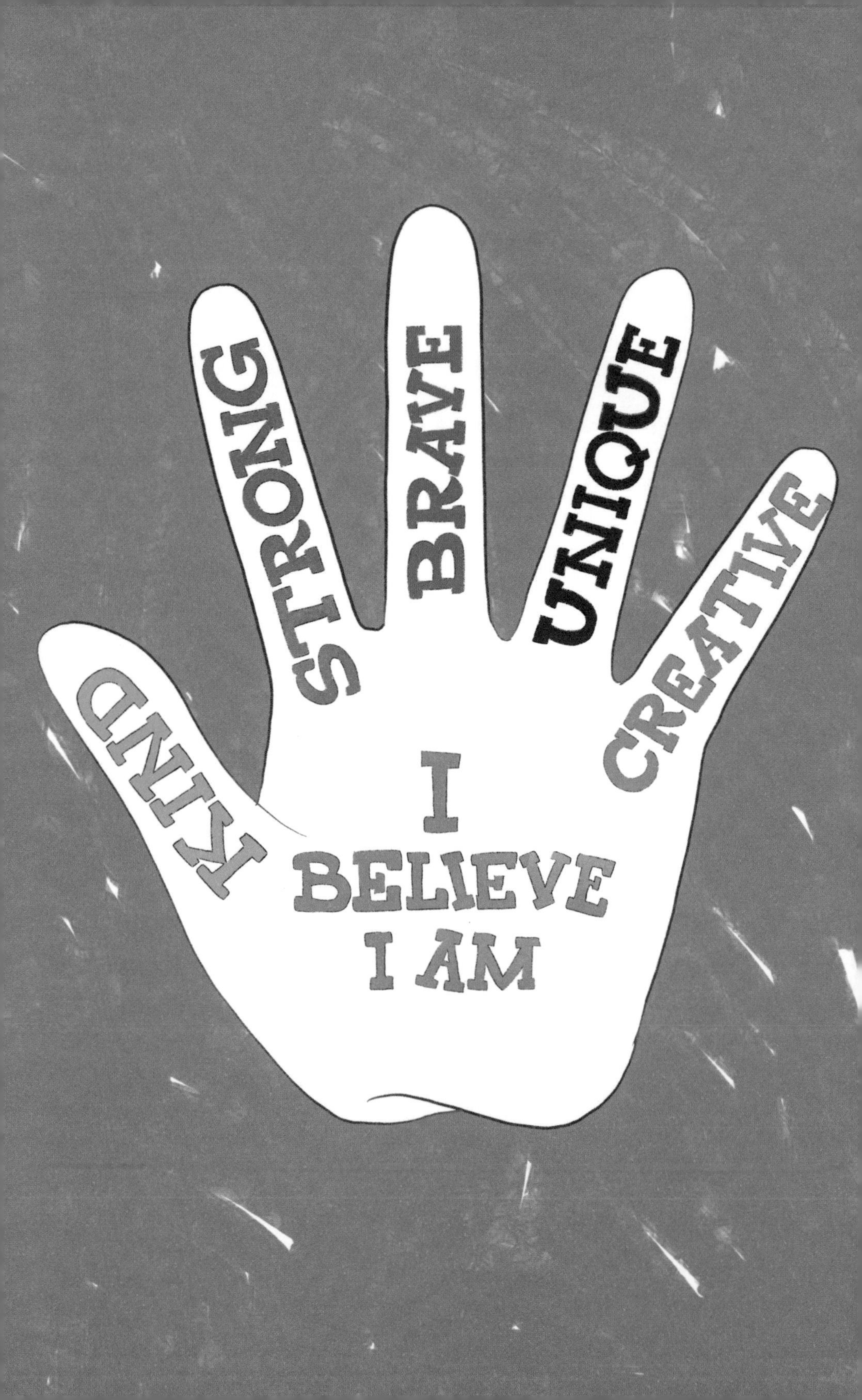
KIND
STRONG
BRAVE
UNIQUE
CREATIVE
I
BELIEVE
I AM

What KIND words can you say to yourself?

Place your palm down below. Use your other hand to trace its outline.

Write "I BELIEVE I AM" in the centre of the outline, and write a positive word that describes you on each finger!

BELIEVE YOU CAN AND YOU'RE HALFWAY THERE

THEODORE ROOSEVELT

Ask your JOURNAL BUDDY to share their most memorable success this year.

NOW IT'S YOUR TURN!

Think about your greatest success this year. Describe it below.

_____

_____

_____

_____

I succeeded because...

☐ I worked hard   ☐ I practised

☐ I asked for help   ☐ I believed in myself

☐ I tried something new ☐ _____

When I succeeded, I felt...

☺ ☹ ☻ ☺ ☺

JUST FOR FUN

Who is the most interesting person to you?

_____

What makes this person so interesting?

_____

_____

✏ Draw or describe that person below.

PART 1

It's normal to be afraid of failing. Almost everyone is afraid to fail at some point. But what if you see your failures and mistakes differently? Not as things to fear but as experiences that help you grow and eventually succeed!

Ask your JOURNAL BUDDY about a mistake they made recently and what they learned from it.

Think about a time when you made a mistake or failed at something. Describe what happened.

_____

_____

_____

What can you learn from this experience?

_____

_____

MISTAKES ARE PROOF that *you* are TRYING

How to Turn Failures into Robots

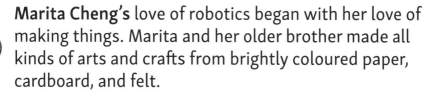

Marita Cheng's love of robotics began with her love of making things. Marita and her older brother made all kinds of arts and crafts from brightly coloured paper, cardboard, and felt.

When Marita reached high school, she went to an engineering camp, where she learned how to build robots out of LEGO bricks, shoot water rockets into the sky, and make a mechatronic catapult!

At university, Marita studied mechanical engineering and electronics, also known as mechatronics. She loved learning how to create useful and interesting kinds of robots. She also noticed hardly any other girls were studying alongside her.

When she went on a university exchange to London, Marita decided to create a robotics club for girls. She arranged the first meeting and welcomed anyone who was interested in robots to come along.

On the big day, Marita waited in the cafeteria for everyone to arrive. She waited and waited, but no one showed up. She sat alone at the empty table and cried. "I'm not going to give up!" Marita thought. And so she tried again.

She arranged a new time to meet. And for the second time, no one showed up. Marita knew that to achieve a different result, she had to try a new strategy.

And with that, she emailed more girls and talked to them one by one. For the third time, she sat at the cafeteria table, and waited. Finally! Four girls showed up, and together they created Robogals London!

To spread word about Robogals, they decided to host an event called "The World's Largest Robot Dance". It was an ambitious idea; they needed 280 people doing the robot dance to break the world record.

Leading up to the event, they created a website, made leaflets and posters, and contacted everyone they could think of who might want to join.

However, on the day of the event, Marita and her three friends waited for 45 minutes in the pouring rain and only one person showed up for the robot dance.

It was disappointing, but Marita was a professional "failure" by now. Instead of getting upset, she laughed about it and began planning her next World's Biggest Robot Dance event, this time in Australia. When that day came, over 360 people showed up and together, they broke the world record!

Robogals has since taught robotics to girls in seventeen cities across four countries.

Marita now owns her own robotics company, Aubot, which makes robots that help people. She loves her work. She loves to try, fail, and try again — every single day!

Think about a robot you want to create. What will it do? Will it help clean your room, play with you, or something else?

_____

_____

_____

Draw your robot below.

PART 2

Did you know mistakes grow your brain?

Something special happens in our brains **only** when we make a mistake. Mistakes cause our brains to spark and grow. In fact, when you get something right, your brain does NOT grow!

What else helps your brain grow?

MOVING YOUR BODY

What's your favourite sport to play?

GETTING ENOUGH SLEEP

What's one thing you like doing before bed?

LEARNING NEW THINGS

What is one new thing you learned recently?

EATING HEALTHY FOODS

What is your favourite healthy snack?

No matter how many times we fail or make a mistake, the important thing is to **try again**.

What happens when an egg drops on the floor? It breaks and stays broken on the floor. And what happens when you drop a ball on the floor? It bounces!

 Ask your JOURNAL BUDDY about a time they were like a ball and bounced back from a failure.

NOW IT'S YOUR TURN!

I bounced back like a ball when _____

_____

_____

Be a Ball!

✓ ✗

SOMETIMES YOU WIN SOMETIMES YOU LEARN

JUST FOR FUN

What is something you want to experience or explore?

_____

Write about it or draw a picture of it below.

PART I

Being persistent means not giving up on something you're learning or doing (even when it's difficult). Sometimes you just need to give yourself and your brain enough time to learn new things. When you're persistent, you can learn anything!

 Ask your JOURNAL BUDDY about a time they worked on something hard and didn't give up. What kind of things kept them going (taking a break, asking for help, or trying a new strategy)?

Think of a time when you were learning something hard. Maybe a time when you even thought about giving up, but you kept on going! Tell the story below.

I was learning _____

It was difficult and I felt...

☐ 🙂 stuck   ☐ 🙁 frustrated

☐ 🙁 angry   ☐ 😄 hopeful

☐ ⚪ _____   ☐ ⚪ _____

I am glad I stayed persistent and didn't give up because

_____

_____

A **River**
CUTS THROUGH **ROCK**

NOT BECAUSE
OF its **POWER**

BUT BECAUSE
OF its

PERSISTENCE

JIM WALKERS

The Boy Who Never Gave Up

Ade Adeptian was born in Nigeria. When he was just six months old, he contracted a disease called polio. This meant Ade wasn't able to walk properly and he had to use special tools called calipers to move around. Ade's mum and dad made the difficult decision to move to London, when he was three years old, in the hope of a brighter future.

On his first day of school, Ade walked into the playground and saw a group of kids playing football. He begged them to let him join in, but they refused. He was limping because of his condition — there was no way they were letting him play! But Ade was determined to convince them. He pleaded with them all day, and at last, they agreed to let him be the goalie.

Ade knew he could prove them all wrong. When the best player in the school blasted the ball towards the net, Ade soared into the air and caught the ball! Ade went from "the weird new kid" to a sporting hero in one afternoon.

One day, Ade saw the Great British Wheelchair Basketball team play at an event and it changed his life. He had never seen anything like it; these basketball players had huge muscles, sporty wheelchairs, and were spinning and swerving around the court like breakdancers on wheels! It was at this moment that Ade decided to become an international wheelchair

basketball player.

Ade's dream of becoming a basketball champion took a lot of persistence. He nearly gave up because of the number of times he tried and failed to make the national team of Great Britain. But Ade had a passion for basketball and he could not be stopped. He was determined to succeed and worked on improving his technique one day at a time.

Ade trained six days a week, shooting 800–900 hoops every single day! He became resilient and wasn't afraid of being rejected any more because he was always trying his best. His failures helped him only train harder, improving his technique one day at a time.

And, finally, Ade was selected to Team Great Britain in the Paralympics! His sports dream began at the age of nine and by the age of 27, he reached his biggest dream. He persisted and never gave up.

In 2004, Ade and his teammates won the bronze medal in Athens. He even scored the winning basket at the Paralympic World Cup, where the team took home the gold medal.

Ade has since used his positive attitude to travel the world, produce documentaries, become a children's TV presenter, and write children's books. He loves inspiring kids to shoot for the stars!

Ade had a very big dream of becoming a basketball champion. He stayed persistent and didn't give up until he had reached his goal!

What is YOUR big dream? Is there anything you want to become, learn, or do?

MY DREAM

Why is this dream important to you?

_____

_____

PART 2

Sometimes when we make a mistake, it just means we haven't learned how to do it YET.

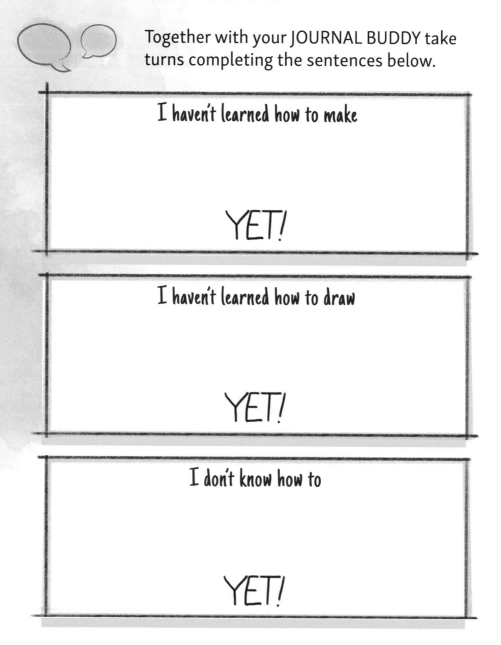

Together with your JOURNAL BUDDY take turns completing the sentences below.

I haven't learned how to make

YET!

I haven't learned how to draw

YET!

I don't know how to

YET!

The "YET" at the end means you are on your way to improving what you are learning.

Imagine you and your friend are working on a comic book. Your friend was drawing and erasing over and over again but only drew the main character below.

They felt discouraged and didn't want to keep going.

Finish your friend's drawing below. You will show how teamwork can help us keep going when we face challenges.

Sometimes when we work on something difficult, we might feel like giving up. But if we take a short break, we can go back to the same activity with more energy and try again!

 Ask your JOURNAL BUDDY about their favourite way to take a break when they're working on something difficult.

NOW IT'S YOUR TURN!

Imagine you're working on something difficult. Your brain or body is getting tired, so you need to take a break.

Tick the ways you like to take a break and add some of your own to the list.

- [ ] Listening to music

- [ ] Colouring

- [ ] Jumping on a trampoline

- [ ] Taking deep breaths

- [ ] _____

- [ ] _____

- [ ] _____

the most
CERTAIN WAY
TO
SUCCEED
is always
TO TRY
JUST ONE
MORE TIME

THOMAS A. EDISON

JUST FOR FUN

What do you most like to create, make, or build?

_____

_____

✏️ Draw your new creation below.

PART 1

It is fun to find things for which you are grateful. You can be grateful for a person, a place, or something else, like a family trip or the sunset. When you remind yourself to be grateful, you are happier, healthier, and more present.

Ask your JOURNAL BUDDY what they are grateful for today.

NOW IT'S YOUR TURN!

Starting with each letter, write down something you're thankful for which begins with that letter.
For example, T — my Toys, H — our House, and so on...

T _____

H _____

A _____

N _____

K _____

F _____

U _____

L _____

be

GRATEFUL

FOR BIG THINGS

FOR SMALL THINGS

AND EVERYTHING

IN BETWEEN

Wong and the Amazing Sun Bears

Wong Siew Te was born in Malaysia, a country known for its amazing wildlife and mighty rainforests.

As a young boy, Wong learned how to nurse baby birds that had fallen from their nests. He soon discovered his passion for bird-watching and always felt grateful for the incredible nature around him.

Wong's love and gratitude for animals inspired him to study wildlife biology. One day, while studying in the USA, Wong met a bear biologist who told him something interesting. In Malaysia, there lives a type of bear called the sun bear, and nobody was studying it at the time.

More importantly, sun bears were in danger! Wong already knew he wanted to dedicate his life to preserving wildlife, so he decided to investigate.

The more Wong learned about sun bears, the more he grew to love them. He discovered how important they were to the ecosystem.

Sun bears keep trees healthy by eating the bugs that feed on the wood. They help new trees grow by spreading seeds throughout the forest with their big claws. When sun bears dig for food, they create homes for rare birds. Wong realised sun bears are like the doctors, farmers, and engineers of the forest!

However, not everyone appreciated the sun bears' work — many people would catch them and keep them in cages as pets.

Wong knew these bears were meant to live in the forest and not as pets, so he decided to take action. He created a conservation centre, a place that protects animals and keeps them safe.

So far, the Sun Bear Conservation Centre has saved 61 sun bears from cruel lives in cages and zoos. Wong and his volunteers teach the bears how to climb trees and find their own food so they are able to live by themselves in the rainforests.

The first sun bear Wong ever saved was a playful bear called Natalie. Natalie's mother had been taken when she was just three months old.

Wong cared for Natalie for the next four years. He played, walked, and climbed with her amongst the trees and helped her become brave enough to meet other bears.

When Natalie had all the skills she needed to live in the wild, Wong released her into the rainforest. He was sad to say goodbye but he knew it was the right thing to do for the ecosystem and for Natalie.

Wong's gratitude for the bears helped him positively impact their lives, which in turn positively impacted his own...because when we do good things for the world, we feel good about ourselves.

Imagine you were volunteering in a conservation centre. What wild animals would you be helping to raise?

Complete the drawing of the conservation centre and include the animals.

PART 2

GRATITUDE SCAVENGER HUNT

1

2

3

4

5

Let's see if you can complete this scavenger hunt from where you are sitting right now.

Look around the room you're in. See how many things you can find from the list below. As you find them, draw them on the previous page.

Something I am grateful for that...

1 I enjoy looking at.

2 I am thankful to have.

3 is my favourite color.

4 is useful to me.

5 I can share with someone else.

 Ask your JOURNAL BUDDY about one good thing that happened to them today and why they're grateful for it.

Describe one good thing that happened to you today and why you're grateful it happened.

_____

_____

_____

How do you feel about today?

What can you do to make tomorrow a super day?

_____

_____

_____

- it's Not -
HAPPY PEOPLE
WHO ARE
thankful

IT'S THANKFUL

PEOPLE WHO ARE
HAPPY

JUST FOR FUN

What are three things (or people) that make you smile?

1. _____

2. _____

3. _____

Draw or describe one or more of them below.

PART 1

Imagine if a rainbow had only one colour. Or if everyone walked, talked, and dressed the same. The world would be a pretty boring place, wouldn't it? When you appreciate your uniqueness and that of others, you become more loving towards yourself and the world.

 Ask your JOURNAL BUDDY to name one unique thing about them.

 **NOW IT'S YOUR TURN!**

What is one unique thing about you?

_____

Draw yourself below wearing a fun and unique outfit.

Be YOURSELF. EVERYONE ELSE IS ALREADY TAKEN.

A World Adventurer

Kira Salak had always known she was different. When she was six years old, she loved spending time in her imaginary world, writing stories by herself.

Kira's parents sent her to boarding school in Wisconsin, USA, where she quickly excelled at sports. To some people, this could have meant a career in professional athletics, but not to Kira. She was good at athletics. However, being an athlete wasn't her dream.

By the time Kira was in her late teens, she knew she wanted to become an explorer and write about her adventures. So instead of continuing her sports training programme, she began travelling the world!

Kira travelled to the giant tribal island of Papua New Guinea — a place where 800 different languages are spoken. Despite many dangers, such as tropical snakes and poisonous bugs, Kira managed to cross Papua New Guinea, all by herself. She became the first American woman ever to achieve this feat.

Just like when she was six years old, Kira wrote about her experiences. The book she wrote launched her dream career as a writer, and her appetite for adventure continued to grow.

Kira's most ambitious trip took her back to Africa. This time, she decided to travel by kayak! Her goal was to kayak the entire Niger River — 600 miles, through five different countries, passing through jungles, deserts, and encountering countless deadly animals.

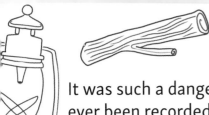

It was such a dangerous journey that no person had ever been recorded doing it before. However, Kira had always lived her life by one important rule: just because something has never been done before doesn't mean it can't be done!

As she kayaked in the searing heat each day, the women from the villages would come to clap and cheer her on. They shouted, "Femme forte!" which in French means "Strong woman!"

But not all journeys are through water, jungles, or deserts. Some journeys take place inside of us. When Kira was 34, tragedy struck, and her brother passed away.

Kira dealt with this in her unique way. She went to her basement and started to write, as she had always done. After one year of tireless writing, Kira emerged with her first novel.

No matter what the world expected from Kira, she would always do things her own way.

Kira's adventurous spirit is what's unique about her. She has travelled the world, learned new languages, and met hundreds of people.

To this day, Kira loves to overcome new challenges and move fearlessly forward!

You can be an adventurer too!

Where would you go? It could be a place you've never been or an imaginary place. Describe and draw it below.

_____

_____

_____

PART 2

All of us have unique strengths and interests, and we like different things.

What about you? Look at the two columns below and circle which you prefer.

I prefer

Saturday	←——→	Sunday
snow	←——→	rain
fruits	←——→	vegetables
coming up with ideas	←——→	figuring out how things work
hiking	←——→	playing at home
finger painting	←——→	colouring pictures
playing music	←——→	dancing
listening to stories	←——→	telling stories

If I made a film
it would be called

If I wrote a book,
it would be about

Something I created
I am proud of

IF I could spend one year
anywhere in the world,

I would go to

Ask your JOURNAL BUDDY if they have met someone who dressed, ate, or spoke differently. What did they like about this person?

Can you think of someone who had something different about them? Maybe it was someone you met or read about.

Who is it?

_____

What did you like about this person?

_____

_____

Can you think of something you had in common with this person?

_____

_____

JUST FOR FUN

Imagine you built your own house. How big or small would it be? What would be unique about it?

_____

_____

✏️ Draw or describe your imaginary house below.

CHALLENGES make you STRONGER

PART 1

Everyone faces big and small challenges every day. Challenges are very important because they help us grow and make us stronger!

 Ask your JOURNAL BUDDY to talk about a challenge they overcame recently.

Think about a challenge you recently faced. For example, an argument with a friend, a difficult test, performance in sports, sickness, or something else.

Describe what happened below.

_____

_____

How did you **feel** when you were going through the challenge? Circle the words which apply and write your own in the open spaces.

disappointed

tired   calm

brave

prepared   scared

YOU CAN'T STOP the WAVES, but You can LEARN HOW to SURF

JON KABAT-ZINN

Never Back Down!

From an early age, **Smriti Mandhana** learned to face challenges head-on. Growing up in India, she loved to play her country's most popular sport: cricket. In fact, she dreamed of becoming a professional cricket player.

Since most professional players are male, she knew it was going to be especially difficult to reach her goal. But she didn't let that discourage her! Smriti knew she could become a great cricket player, as long as she embraced every challenge she faced.

Smriti grew up in a small city called Sangli, known for its sugar cane and spice fields but not for its cricket players!

At the age of five, Smriti regularly walked to the cricket nets with her father and older brother to watch them practise. Smriti's job was to collect the balls and, as a reward, they would let her hit 10 balls at the end of each day.

As her brother began to play professionally, she became even more inspired to keep practising. Smriti practised alongside her brother endlessly until she was finally chosen for her state's u15 (under 15 years old) cricket team. She was just nine years old!

Having been chosen to play with older kids was a challenge, but it would ultimately make Smriti a better player.

ARABIAN SEA

INDIA

Sangli

Smriti continued to dream of one day playing professional cricket in India but knew it wouldn't be an easy goal to reach. There are one billion people living in India and only 11 people on the national cricket team!

Smriti used this challenge as her motivation; she would always wake up early for cricket practise before school, then go for a final practise at night, just before the sunset. Then, at 11 years old, Smriti was selected to play for Maharashtra's u19 professional team.

She faced many challenges on her journey towards becoming a professional athlete. She listened to her coaches, kept making an effort, and improved her performance day by day.

At the age of 17, Smriti became the first Indian woman to score 200 in a one-day cricket match. In 2018, she was voted the world's best female cricketer of the year. She is the most successful cricketer in her family and her brother now fetches the cricket balls for her to hit when she plays!

Smitri's determination to improve every day means she is always seeking challenges. She once said, "No one ever thought that a girl from Sangli would ever play for India — challenge accepted, and completed!"

Smriti had a very big goal and overcame lots of challenges on her way to achieving it.

Can you think of your BIG goal — something you would be very proud to become, do, or achieve? Describe or draw it below.

What might get in the way of you achieving your goal?

_____

_____

Who could help you overcome this challenge?

_____

CHALLENGES make you STRONGER

PART 2

Our roots keep us standing strong

We can think of our lives as trees. The loving adults, teachers, friends, our thoughts, values, and even pets are **roots** which keep us standing strong. Challenges are like the **wind** in the trees. Trees sway but keep standing tall and strong as long as their roots are deep.

Draw your life tree. On the roots, draw people, things, animals, thoughts, and values that make you feel loved and supported. These roots will keep you standing strong when challenges arise and the wind starts blowing.

Think about a problem or challenge you're facing at the moment. It could be a struggle with learning something new, a difficult school assignment, an argument with someone, or something else. Describe it below.

Challenge

_____

_____

 Together with your JOURNAL BUDDY, think of ways you can overcome this challenge. All ideas count! Write them down below.

Solutions

1. _____

2. _____

3. _____

4. _____

5. _____

Circle the one solution you're going to try.

I AM
THANKFUL
FOR my STRUGGLE
because WITHOUT IT,
I WOULDN'T HAVE
STUMBLED
UPON my
STRENGTH.
ALEXANDRA ELLE

JUST FOR FUN

Think of a funny moment in your life. Draw a comic strip about it below.

PART I

We learn and get better at things by making an effort. Making an effort means practising, working hard, and trying different strategies.

Ask your JOURNAL BUDDY about a time when they had to make a big effort. Did they use different strategies? Did they succeed in the end?

NOW IT'S YOUR TURN!

Describe a time when you make a big effort.

_____

_____

_____

How did you feel during the process?

How did you feel in the end?

SUCCESS
is the SUM
OF SMALL
EFFORTS
REPEATED
day IN & day OUT

ROBERT COLLIER

Effort the Size of Everest

Growing up, **Edurne Pasaban** was a true mountain girl. She loved to walk, run, and even climb up the rocky peaks near her house in the hills of northern Spain.

She loved the feeling of climbing higher each time and looking back at the tiny houses dotted across the valley below. By the time she was 14, Edurne had joined a mountaineering club and was already climbing with adults.

As a reward for her hard work, Edurne was chosen for the adventure of a lifetime — to climb a 6,000-metre peak (equivalent to 60 rugby pitches) in South America!

When she wasn't mountain climbing, she was competing in triathlons to increase her core strength and endurance. Swimming, cycling, running...Edurne did everything she could to prepare her body for the toughest challenges.

Edurne became a world-class mountain climber, climbing the world's highest peak, Mount Everest. After more years of hard work, Edurne became the first woman to climb 14 of the world's tallest mountains.

Edurne then decided it was time to conquer Mount Everest again. During the team's preparation for the expedition, Edurne felt strong. They had done many months of hard training.

If the trip was successful, Edurne was going to be the first woman to climb all 14 of the world's tallest mountains without extra oxygen (many climbers need to use oxygen tanks to help them breathe due to the lower oxygen levels at higher altitudes).

However, as the team reached the final part of the climb, two members of her team became ill. As team leader, Edurne made the decision to pause the expedition so her teammates could rest and receive extra oxygen. At this point, she was left with a difficult decision: should she continue climbing to achieve the world record?

Edurne was so close to the peak and could see other expeditions reaching the top. But she decided to focus all of her efforts on saving her teammates.

Her team helped the two sick climbers down the mountain, where they were taken to safety. Even though Edurne didn't succeed in reaching the peak, all her efforts gained her something else equally important — her teammates were safe.

After many years of climbing the world's highest peaks, Edurne remains an ambitious climber who puts all her effort into every expedition. Her new goal is to cross the Himalayan mountains on foot. She continues to reach for new heights every day and take care of her teammates!

If you were to climb Mount Everest, what are the top three things you would take with you? A waterproof rucksack, warm clothing, your favourite snacks, or something else?
Write down and draw your top three things below.

ITEM

DRAWING

☐ _____

☐ _____

☐ _____

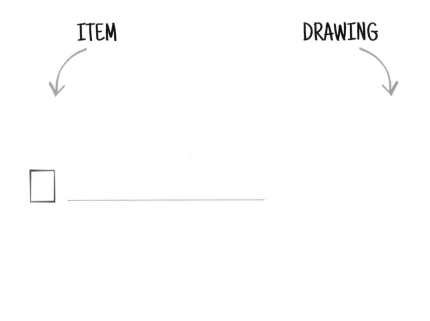

PART 2

What happens when you do something over and over again?

Imagine you are standing in front of a big field of tall grass and you need to cross to the other side. The first time you try, you might have to work your way through, but you will get there.

This is difficult!

When you do it again, it becomes a little bit easier. And each time you cross the field, you find it becomes easier until you have created a clear path.

I've done this many times, it is easy now!

The same thing happens inside your **brain**. The cells inside your brain create a new path or pathway between each other when you learn something new.

Every time you practise, a special signal travels along this pathway.

The more you practise, the easier it is for the signal to travel because the pathway becomes clearer.

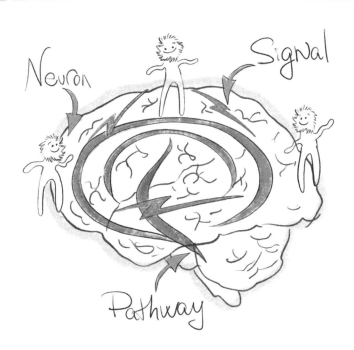

Neuron

Signal

Pathway

What is one thing you need to practise to form a pathway in your brain?

When you work on something, it is important to do your best and take pride in your work.

 Ask your JOURNAL BUDDY when they did their best and felt proud of their work.

NOW IT'S YOUR TURN!

Describe a time when you did your best and felt proud of your work.

I did my best when_____

_____

_____

When I do my best I...

☐ ask questions ☐ keep going when it's difficult

☐ take my time ☐ ask for help

☐ check my work ☐ _____

When I do my best I feel...

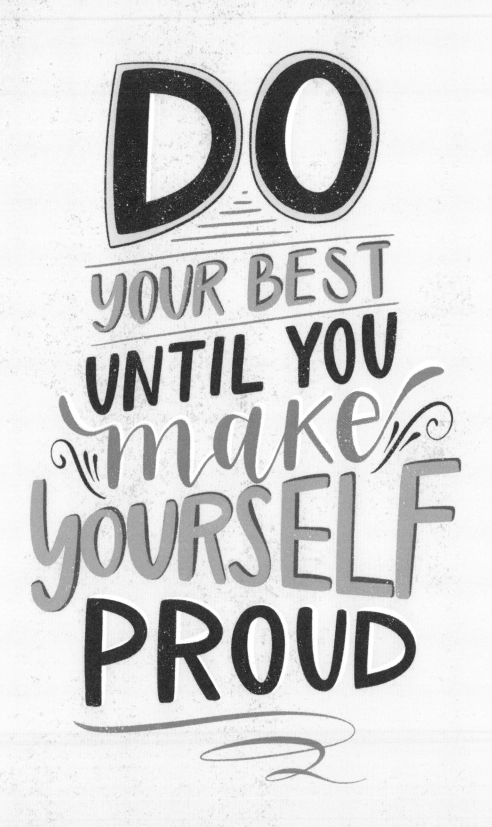

JUST FOR FUN

If you could throw a party for your friends and family,
what would it be like?

🖊 Draw or describe your party below.

PART 1

Learning helps us discover the world and makes our lives more interesting. It's fun to learn something new because then you have the opportunity to share it with or teach it to someone else.

Ask your JOURNAL BUDDY about one new thing they learned today.

What is one new thing you learned today?

_____

🖉 Draw or describe it below.

I HAVE NO SPECIAL Talents

I am only

PASSIONATELY CURIOUS

ALBERT EINSTEIN

Explore Your Universe

When **Chris Hadfield** was 10 years old, he made the decision to become an astronaut.

Chris loved to read. He read books about the moon, about rockets...anything about outer space! Chris especially loved reading science fiction and comic books because they inspired him to dream of truly out-of-this-world things. Chris was dreaming of the unknown...of a future in space!

When Canada first formed a space agency, Chris was excited! The ideas he had been reading about, and dreaming of, were becoming a reality. People were really leaving Earth and going into outer space.

Being an astronaut involves a lot of things some people find scary and dangerous. But Chris knew as long as he prepared himself and learned everything he could about his mission, there was no reason to be scared.

When you take time to learn, you can feel calm, confident, and in control.

One of the ways Chris prepared himself to become an astronaut was by learning Russian. Chris knew he would be working with a lot of Russian astronauts, and it was important to be able to communicate with them.

Russian is a complicated language, but Chris knew any kind of learning can be divided into small steps.

Because of his dedication, Chris became the first Canadian to walk in space. On their first mission, Chris and his crew orbited around the world sixteen times per day!

Chris got to see Earth from a whole new perspective. He saw beautiful sunrises and sunsets every 45 minutes, and experienced the constantly changing beauty of the world from a great, great distance.

Chris' love of learning goes further than outer space. He takes great joy and inspiration from learning about all sorts of things: new languages, health, music, and creativity. He is currently learning how to play the trombone.

It took 23 years for Chris to fulfil his dream of becoming an astronaut. Every step of the way, he was learning to reach his goal.

And the best part? He found happiness in the journey towards his goal, not just the end result. Chris made sure he enjoyed every stepping stone on his learning path, no matter how small.

The biggest lesson Chris learned from leaving Earth is to stay curious. The universe is bigger than we can possibly imagine, and it's waiting for us to explore it all!

What are some things you are curious about? Draw or write about them below.

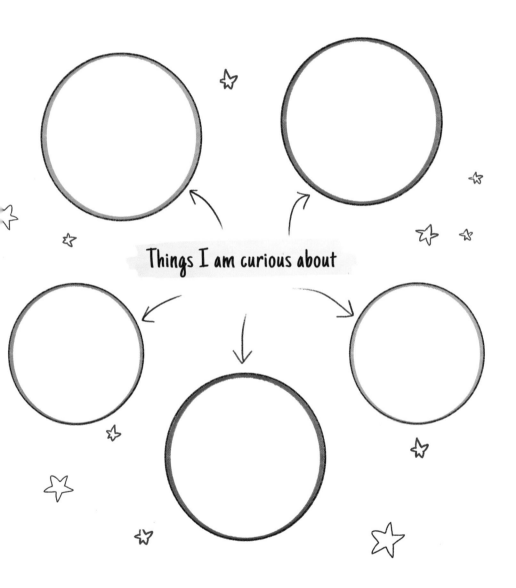

Things I am curious about

PART 2

How does learning change your brain?

When we are learning something new it might feel hard and uncomfortable...

That uncomfortable feeling is your brain trying to learn.

Being uncomfortable is really important because this is what makes our squishy brains change to a different shape, a bit like clay.

If you help your brain and push through the hard parts, your brain will reshape itself.

And you will get better at what you're learning!

What is one thing you recently learned that made your brain work really hard? Write about it or draw it below.

Ask your JOURNAL BUDDY what subject they would teach if they were a teacher.

NOW IT'S YOUR TURN!

What is one thing you can already teach someone?

_____

What subject would you teach if you were a teacher?

_____

You as a teacher

GIVE *your* BRAIN *time to* LEARN

JUST FOR FUN

Draw or describe five things that make you laugh.

PART 1

Did you know you already have one big superpower? It's the superpower of kindness! You can make someone's day better, and make them feel instantly good, simply by being kind to them.

 Ask your JOURNAL BUDDY to tell you about a kind thing they have done for someone recently.

NOW IT'S YOUR TURN!

Think about a time you did something kind for someone. Write what happened below.

I was kind when _____

_____

_____ .

_____

When I do something kind for someone, I feel...

When someone says "thank you" to me, I feel...

IN A WORLD WHERE you CAN BE ANYTHING BE KIND

Find Your Secret Superpower

Tina Hovsepian has always loved to create. Growing up in Los Angeles, Tina saw lots of beautiful people with fancy cars and big houses. She loved fashion and dreamt of designing mountains of colourful clothes.

As she got older, Tina discovered something else about the city she lived in. She saw many people sleeping on the streets. Many of these homeless people had nowhere else to go, and no one to help them. Seeing these ordinary people sleeping on the streets made Tina feel sad.

Tina also noticed pedestrians avoiding homeless people. They would cross the road or ignore them when they asked for help.

One person who did not do this was Tina's auntie. She would always stop and chat with the homeless. She listened to them, and asked questions like, "Are you okay? Can I get you something to eat? How can I help you?" Tina found this very inspiring.

Tina's auntie taught her the importance of kindness; you can make someone feel good in an instant, just by being kind to them. This was the moment Tina discovered kindness was like a superpower!

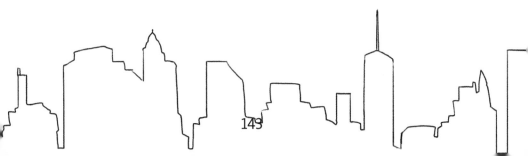

143

In her later years, Tina decided to study something that could help others: architecture. For her final university project, she decided to help the homeless.

She wanted to create inexpensive, easy-to-build shelters for anyone who needed somewhere safe to sleep. Using cardboard, Tina experimented with ways to fold the material so it could pop open in seconds and transform into a small space, providing privacy and warmth.

After many months of trial and error, Tina finally found the perfect design. She followed the rules of the ancient Japanese art called origami, and named her idea Cardborigami, because that's what it was: cardboard and origami!

Thanks to Tina's simple creation, she has been able to help hundreds of homeless people by providing Cardborigami houses for them to sleep in.

Through her amazing skills and ideas, Tina showed anyone can turn kindness into their superpower. You just need to put yourself in someone else's shoes and imagine how they are feeling. Maybe you could help them by listening, chatting, or even with a smile.

You can change someone's world with your kindness superpower, just like Tina did!

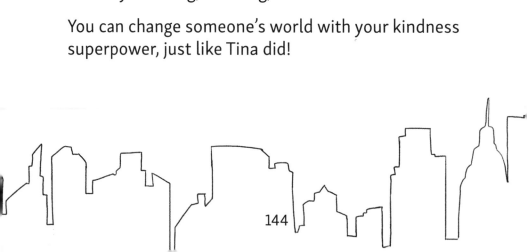

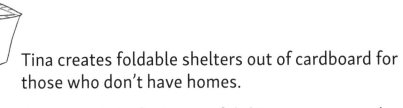

Tina creates foldable shelters out of cardboard for those who don't have homes.

Can you think of other useful things you can make out of cardboard? A plate, a car, a hat, or anything else?

Write down and draw your ideas below.

IDEAS   DRAWINGS

1. _____

2. _____

3. _____

Can you find an empty cardboard box to turn one of your ideas into the real thing?

PART 2

You can share your kindness every day by showing others you care. Finish the sentences in boxes below.

I can ask, "Can I help?" when someone

I can ask, "Would you like to join?" when someone

I can ask, "Is everything alright?" when someone

Use the **Kindness Tracker** on the next page to track your kind acts. Every time you do something kind for someone, colour in a piece of the heart. See how quickly you manage to colour in your heart!

My Kindness Tracker

Day I started the tracker: _____

 Ask your JOURNAL BUDDY how they show kindness to themselves.

What are three ways you can show kindness to **yourself**?

For example, you can say something encouraging to yourself or ask someone for help when you need it. Write down your ideas below.

3 ways I can show kindness to myself

 _____

_____

_____

When I am kind to myself, I feel...

Be Somebody WHO MAKES EVERYONE FEEL LIKE A Somebody

ROBBY NOVAK

JUST FOR FUN

Write about your favourite memory with one of your friends. What happened?

_____

_____

_____

✎ Draw the two of you together below.

PART I

Everyone can make a difference in the world, and you can too! For example, you can solve a problem, help someone in need, or take care of our planet.

 Ask your JOURNAL BUDDY to name someone who is making a difference in the world.

NOW IT'S YOUR TURN!

Think of someone who is making a difference in the world. It could be a teacher, family member, friend, or someone famous.

Who is it? _____

How are they making a difference in the world?

_____

_____

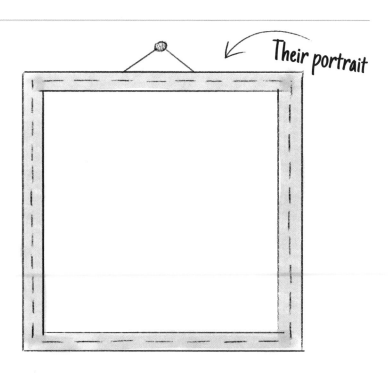

Their portrait

If you always GIVE you will always HAVE

CHINESE PROVERB

Change the World with a Single Seed

When **Kyle Kornack** first experienced the fierce heat of the wildfires near his house, he couldn't believe what he was seeing; the flames had destroyed hundreds of trees in minutes.

It became so hot, he felt like there was a volcano erupting in his backyard and the ash began falling on his roof. The wildfires on the hill were becoming more frequent and ferocious and the trees were disappearing.

A lot of people don't think about the importance of trees but Kyle knows just how necessary they are. Every single tree in the world provides us with oxygen. Trees also create shelter and food for wildlife.

Kyle thought of hundreds of ways trees make a difference in the world and it got him thinking...maybe he could make a difference, just like them!

When Kyle got involved in learning about fish and wildlife at a local club, he learned about sustainability. Kyle discovered there were ways he could preserve the environment by using less plastic, eating locally grown foods, and reusing items instead of discarding.

Kyle became so passionate about the new skills he was learning, he decided to go to university to find out how he could make an even bigger difference.

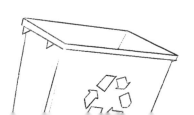

After university, Kyle felt a little frustrated. He spent five years studying environmental problems, but he didn't find any solutions!

In class, Kyle learned that daily activities like using transportation or electricity make a "carbon footprint" or an impact on the environment.

He also learned that "carbon offsets" were ways to balance out the footprint by doing something good for the environment. Suddenly, Kyle had an idea: the GreenGas card — a simple credit card with a lot of power!

Every time someone uses their GreenGas card to buy petrol, Kyle's team and its partners plant a tree. This way, when people drive cars they can offset their negative impact on the environment.

Thanks to Kyle's love of nature, hundreds of trees have already been planted along the Mississippi River. The trees help to absorb carbon emissions, create wildlife habitat, and maintain healthy soil.

Kyle believes we can all make a difference in the world, no matter how small. His top tip? Spend more time in nature and plant a tree of your own!

Organise your own tree planting event! Finish and colour the flyer below. In the middle, draw the type of tree you would like to plant.

Tree Planting

Organised by _____

DATE _____ TIME _____

PLACE _____

Discuss with your JOURNAL BUDDY how you can organise a tree planting event in your community.

PART 2

Design a T-shirt for a cause!

1. Find an organisation that does good in the world. For example, a charity or your local library.

   What is it?_____

2. Imagine they need help with designing a T-shirt for their supporters to wear. You've volunteered to help!

3. Use the next page to create your design. Remember to include an inspirational message on the T-shirt.

Find out if this organisation has a website.

Does the website include ways to help? Take a look and discuss with your JOURNAL BUDDY how **you** can help.

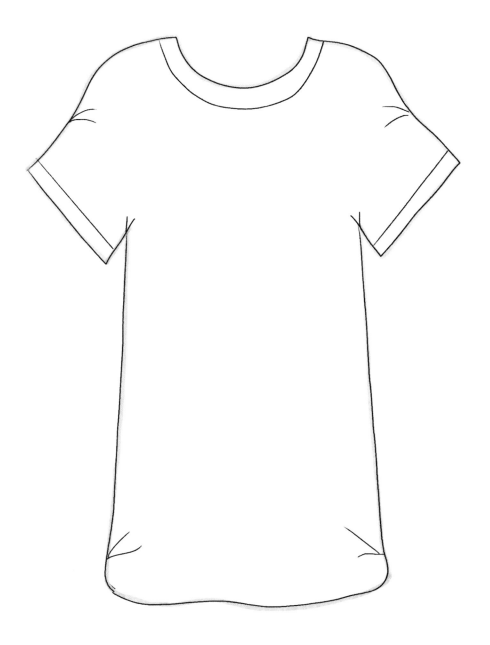

Artist's name: _____

Ask your JOURNAL BUDDY to name one thing they can do to improve their local community.

NOW IT'S YOUR TURN!

Check the boxes of things you could do and add your own ideas. Then select one thing you will do **this week** and circle it.

☐ Organise a beach or park cleanup with friends.

☐ Bake biscuits to sell for a local charity.

☐ Donate nearly new toys and clothes.

☐ Make cards for the elderly in a nursing home.

☐ Volunteer at a community garden.

☐ Volunteer at your local animal shelter.

☐ Do housework for a sick friend or neighbour.

☐ _____

☐ _____

☐ _____

WE CAN CHANGE THE WORLD AND MAKE IT A BETTER PLACE

NELSON MANDELA

JUST FOR FUN

Imagine you woke up and you were living in a different time period (for example, in ancient times or sometime in the future). Which time period would it be?

 Think how different life would be in that time period. Draw or describe it below.

Make your own poster!

By now you have all the pieces to create your own poster. Cut out the colouring pages from each chapter and assemble in any order you like. Glue or tape the pages onto a poster-size paper. Hang it up on a wall where you can see it often.

the BIG Life KIDS PODCAST

Two best friends, Zara and Leo, are flying their magical vehicle Believemobile around the world to tell stories of remarkable people who chase their dreams and

never give up!

Listen to the full stories from this journal and discover how to be the best version of yourself!

Go to biglifejournal.com/podcast to listen!

Listen to the podcast and draw the two main characters, Zara and Leo, below.

The Big Life Journal — Teen Edition teaches tweens & teens they have the power to decide who they are...and take charge of who they're becoming.

A perfect gift for ages 11 and above!

This guided journal gets tweens & teens excited about the limitless possibilities ahead because, with a growth mindset, they can go after anything!

Go to biglifejournal.com

- Discover the power of mindset

- Learn how to handle negative self-talk

- Create and plan out goals

- Learn how to overcome challenges

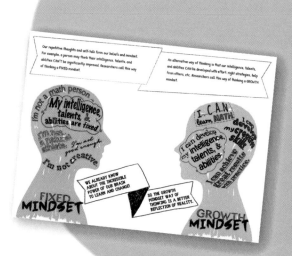

The Teacher Guide is available for teachers and homeschoolers.

Go to biglifejournal.com

Acknowledgments

A big THANK-YOU to our large community of parents and educators. We drew lots of ideas for this journal from their feedback and poll responses.

This journal would not be possible without the help of our amazing Big Life Journal TEAM! They relentlessly tested the activities with their children, provided feedback, and helped us make decisions.

A thank-you to our extended review and editing team for their guidance. The team included several teachers, parents, homeschoolers, and a doctor of psychology.

Finally, special thanks to Dr. Carol Dweck for her body of work on growth mindset theory.

Written by Alexandra Eidens. **Stories** by Sarah Cyrano. **Design** by Sarah Saiyara and Emilia Jesenska. **Quote design** by Tania June and Aleksandra Korableva. **Illustrations** by Sarah Saiyara and Aleksandra Korableva. **Cover** by Tania June.